Around Scottish Borders

Contents

Introduction	2
Sir Walter Scott	4
Towns, villages and the countryside of the Borders	6
Abbeys of the Borders	10
Map	16
Castles, Houses and Gardens	18
Border Forests	22
Common Ridings	23
Museums and other places to visit	24
Walking in the Borders	28
The Southern Upland Way	29
The Woollen Industry	30
General information	inside back cover

Below: *St Mary's Loch, popular with sailors.* **Ci-dessous:** *le loch St Mary's.* **Unten:** *St. Mary's Loch ist bei Seglern beliebt.*

Introduction

For many people, 'the Borders' is the area they rush through on the way to Edinburgh and thence to the Highlands – yet in doing so they miss seeing one of Scotland's loveliest regions. Maybe the countryside is not, at first sight, as spectacular as that further north, but what the hills lack in height, they make up in sheer presence, with the Cheviots dominating the south, the Moorfoots and Lammermuirs the north and the three Eildon peaks constantly on the horizon in the central area.

The countryside also offers a great variety of different habitats: not only are there rugged moorlands, but also lush pastures in the river valleys; forests provide sheltered habitats for a rich range of wildlife, while the Border towns are the home of a flourishing textile industry and the famous knitwear and tweeds of Scotland.

Rivers water the region liberally – the great Tweed itself, the waters of Yarrow, Jed and Ettrick, Blackadder, Eden, Eddleston and Whiteadder; their names alone conjure up images of bubbling springs alive with salmon, trout and coarse fish. There is even a 'Highland' loch – St Mary's, with the little Loch of the Lowes close by, while Talla and Megget Reservoirs offer additional fishing opportunities.

For centuries, this land saw constant turmoil and strife as raiding parties fought to and fro across the unsettled boundary dividing Scotland from England. The many ruined castles dotted across the landscape and the remains of once-proud but still beautiful abbeys show the scars of those times, thankfully long past, while stately mansions declare the peace and prosperity of later centuries.

In this book, we have tried to show as many different aspects of life in the Borders as space allows. Grid references in brackets (e.g. B6) refer to the map on the centre pages, which indicates many of the principal places of interest to visit, while useful addresses appear inside the back cover. We hope you enjoy your visit.

La région des « Borders » (Border signifie frontière) est en général une région que l'on traverse à la hâte en route pour Edimbourg et les Highlands. Elle mérite pourtant que les visiteurs s'y attardent car c'est l'une des plus jolies régions d'Ecosse. Le paysage n'est sans doute pas aussi spectaculaire que celui du Nord du pays mais les collines des « Borders », d'altitude modeste, ne manquent pas de caractère, leur horizon dominé par les Cheviots au Sud, les Moorfoots et Lammermuirs au Nord et les trois sommets des Eildon au centre.

La région est variée également sur le plan des terrains: landes sauvages succèdent aux riches pâturages des vallées; les forêts abritent une faune abondante tandis que dans les villes une industrie textile florissante s'est implantée avec notamment les célèbres Tweeds écossais.

Les nombreuses rivières – Tweed, Yarrow, Jed, Ettrick, Blackadder, Eden, Eddleston et Whiteadder – sont riches en saumons, truites, gardons, ombres, brochets et perches. On trouve même un « vrai » loch comme dans les Highlands (St Mary's). Par ailleurs, Lowes, loch de plus petite taille et deux réservoirs (Talla et Megget) offrent leurs eaux au plus grand plaisir des pêcheurs.

Au cours des siècles cette région fut dévastée par des troupes de tous bords se battant pour la frontière mal délimitée entre l'Angleterre et l'Ecosse. Les châteaux en ruines parsemés par toute la région témoignent de ce passé agité ainsi que les restes d'abbayes qui connurent leur heure de gloire. Quelques grandes demeures attestent de la paix et prospérité des siècles suivants.

Dans cet ouvrage nous avons tenté de représenter tous les aspects de la vie dans les « Borders » dans les limites de l'espace imparti. Les numéros entre parenthèses (par exemple B6) renvoient au plan situé au milieu du livre. Ce plan indique les principales attractions et endroits à visiter, tandis que l'on trouvera une liste d'adresses utiles à la fin du guide. Nous vous souhaitons une agréable visite.

Viele Reisende auf dem Weg nach Edinburgh und dem Hochland fahren ohne anzuhalten durch das „Grenzland" und verpassen so eine der schönsten Gegenden Schottlands. Die Landschaft ist vielleicht nicht so atemberaubend wie weiter nördlich, aber die Cheviot Berge im Süden, die Moorfoots und Lammermuirs im Norden und die drei Eildongipfel in der Mitte sind überaus beeindruckend.

Hier findet man rauhe Moore und fruchtbares Weideland und Wälder mit einer Vielfalt von Wild. Die Grenzlandstädte sind Zentrum einer blühenden Textilindustrie und des berühmten schottischen Tweeds.

Flüsse wie der große Tweed, die Wasser des Yarrow, Jed und Ettrick, Blackadder, Eden, Eddleston und Whiteadder durch – ziehen die Gegend. Ihre Namen beschwören Bilder sprudelnder Quellen mit reichen Fischgründen. Ein „Hochland" Loch, St. Mary's, und die

Talla und Megget Reservoire bieten weitere Möglichkeiten zum Angeln.

Die vielen Burgruinen und Überreste einst stolzer, immer noch imposanter Abteien lassen die jahrhundertelangen Kämpfe und Unruhen zwischen England und Schottland in dieser Gegend erkennen, während die vielen Herrenhäuser auf den Frieden und Wohlstand späterer Jahrhunderte deuten.

Dieses Buch soll so viele Seiten des Lebens im „Grenzland" zeigen, wie uns der Platz erlaubt. Gitterangaben in Klammern (z.B. B6) verweisen auf die Karte auf den Mittelseiten mit den interessantesten Orten zur Besichtigung. Nützliche Adressen werden auf der inneren Rückseite angegeben.

Wir hoffen, daß Sie Ihren Besuch genießen.

Above: *Neidpath Castle, on the north bank of the River Tweed.*
Ci-dessus: *Neidpath Castle, sur la rive Nord de la Tweed.*
Oben: *Burg Neidpath am Nordufer des Tweedflusses.*

Sir Walter Scott

Sir Walter Scott, writer and poet, was born in Edinburgh on 15 August 1771, but spent much of his early childhood at his grandparents' Borders farm near Kelso. There he learned to love the Border ballads and legends which later reappeared in many of his published works. He attended Edinburgh's Royal High School, then at the age of twelve entered Edinburgh University. He was called to the Bar as an Advocate in 1792.

In 1797 Scott married Margaret Charlotte Charpentier, daughter of a French refugee. Two years later he was appointed Sheriff-Depute of Selkirkshire and at about the same time started to collect the old Border ballads in earnest. The first two volumes of his collection were published in 1802 and a third in 1803.

In 1804 the family (Scott now had a son and two daughters – a second son was born in 1805) leased Ashiestiel, on the Tweed near Selkirk (C4), and the following year Scott achieved fame for the first time with the publication of his narrative poem *The Lay of the Last Minstrel*. Such was the success of this work that Scott decided to devote most of his time to writing. In 1806 he was appointed Clerk of the Court of Session, which removed any financial pressures.

He wrote early in the morning, starting at six o'clock and continuing for three or four hours. By 1812 he had published his *Life of Dryden* and two more narrative poems, *Marmion* and *The Lady of the Lake* (which made the Trossachs in Perthshire famous overnight). The *Waverley* series of historical novels began to appear in 1814, although Scott only acknowledged he was the author in 1827.

In 1811, Scott purchased a property then called Cartleyhole, later to be renamed Abbotsford, on the banks of the Tweed near Melrose (*left*, C4). The original house was demolished in 1822 and a new mansion erected, filled with treasures collected by Scott or given to him as gifts over the years. His study is shown *above*. In 1820, Scott was created a Baronet.

Disaster struck in 1826: his publishers, Ballantynes, went bankrupt. Scott saw it as a personal duty to earn sufficient money by his writing to pay off the debts, and by extraordinary efforts over the next five years much of the debt was paid. His *Life of Napoleon*, *Tales of a Grandfather* and *History of Scotland* appeared during this period. The incessant toil took its toll, and on 21 September 1832 Scott died at Abbotsford; he was buried at Dryburgh Abbey, in the heart of his beloved Borders.

Towns, villages and the countryside of the Borders

Set among hills, river valleys and pastures, even the most industrialised of Border towns – Hawick and Galashiels – have little villages close by and countryside within walking distance. This close interlinking of the urban and the rural is one of the great charms of the Borders.

Travelling due south from Edinburgh, one reaches historic Peebles (B3), on the banks of the Tweed. With its handsome old buildings and fine stone bridge (fifteenth century, originally timber-built and stone-clad, with splendid silver dolphin lamp-posts embellishing its parapets) Peebles contains much of interest. Among those associated with the town are publishers and printers Robert and William Chambers, and John Buchan, the novelist who wrote *The 39 Steps* (he was born at Tweedsmuir). West Linton (B3), north-west of Peebles, is an attractive little village once famous for its stone-masons. Lady Gifford's Well, in the village, is surmounted by her carved stone effigy dating from 1666. Further west along the Tweed from Peebles lies Drumelzier where, according to one legend, Merlin the wizard lies buried.

Following the Tweed east, the surrounding countryside shows cultivated fields giving way to moorland on the higher slopes, with mixed woodland landscaped by the Forestry Commission – at Glentress forest trails have been laid out. Innerleithen (B4) was a spa town in the eighteenth century (St Ronan's Well, from which visitors used to 'drink the waters', can still be seen) and later the site of one of the first weaving-mills. At Walkerburn, just beyond the town, is a fascinating Museum of Woollen Textiles. From Innerleithen, the B709 branches south to beautiful St Mary's Loch (C3); Tibbie Shiel's Inn, on the spit of land between this loch and the Loch of the Lowes, was well known to

Right: *Peebles;* **below:** *the River Tweed at Yair Bridge, near Selkirk.*
A droite: *Peebles;* **ci-dessous:** *la Tweed à Yair Bridge, près de Selkirk.*
Rechts: *Peebles;* **unten:** *der Fluß Tweed an der Yairbrücke bei Selkirk.*

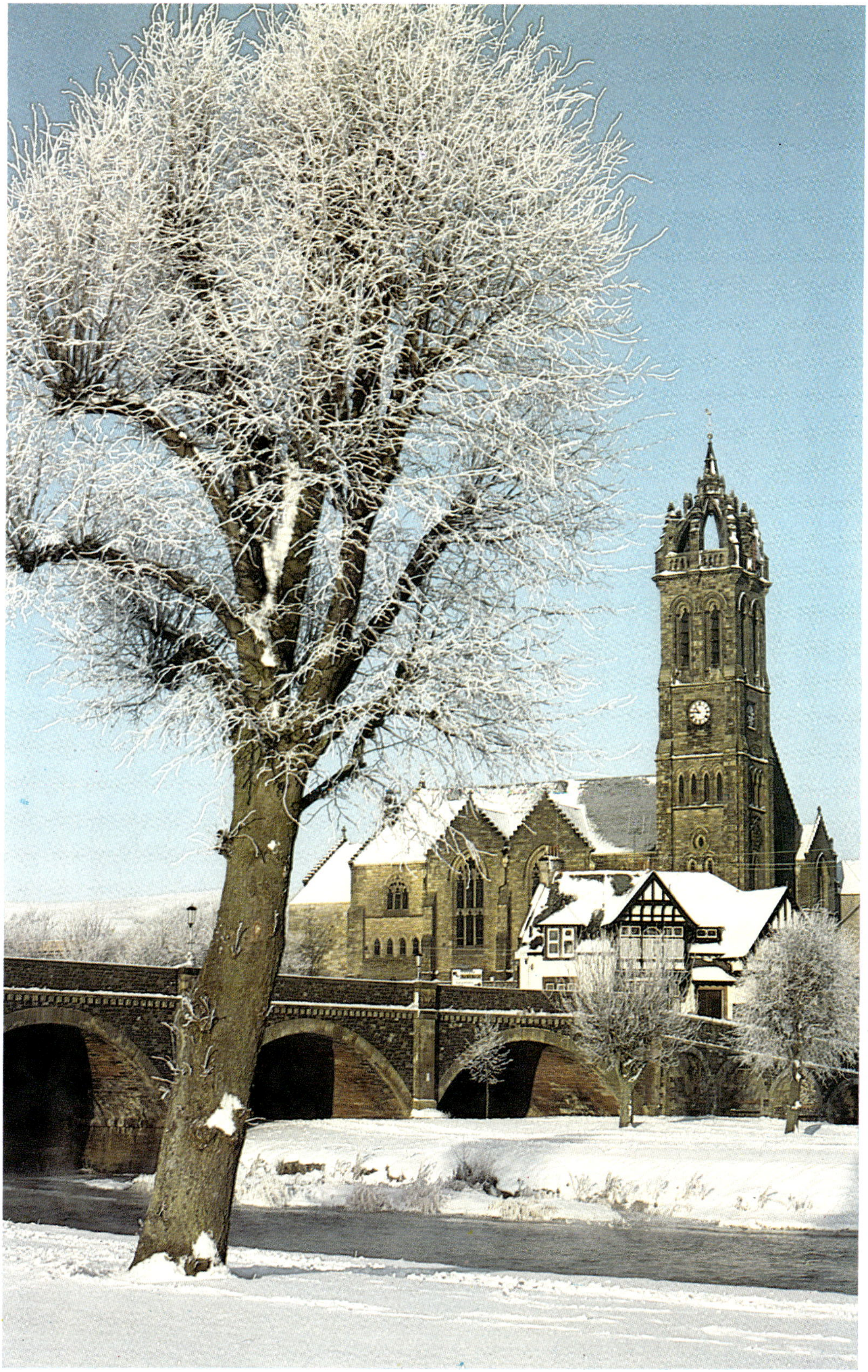

Sir Walter Scott. Just over the regional border to the west is Moffat, a pleasant spa town now popular with tourists, and an important woollen centre.

Galashiels (B4) is more industrialised than some other Border towns and is one of the region's main commercial centres; the Scottish College of Textiles sited in the town is famous. North of Galashiels lies Lauder (B4), an ancient burgh, with the Town Hall dominating the main street, and an attractive church. South lies Selkirk (C4), once famous for its shoe industry – the inhabitants are called 'souters' (shoemakers) to this day. Sir Walter Scott was once Sheriff of this important mill town and a statue of him stands in the market-place. Also associated with Selkirk is the explorer and missionary Mungo Park, born at Foulshiels in 1771.

Hawick (C4), in Teviotdale still further south, has the largest population of any Border town and is also industrialised, being proud of its place as a centre of the knitwear industry. Hawick was frequently attacked by Border raiders and a statue in the main street commemorates a victory against an English raiding party.

In Liddesdale, at the southernmost tip of the region, is eighteenth-century Newcastleton (D4), built as a handloom-weaving centre by the third Duke of Buccleuch.

Returning now to the Tweed as it flows on eastwards, the visitor reaches the heart of 'Scott Country' at Melrose (C4). Abbotsford, Scott's much-loved home, lies to the west, while the Eildon Hills, at which he gazed across the Tweed Valley from a spot still called Scott's View, rise eastwards. Melrose developed around its abbey, now a picturesque ruin, where, tradition relates, the heart of Robert the Bruce lies buried. This tranquil little town, with its well-kept houses and shops, is now a tourist centre for the area.

Travelling on towards Newtown St Boswells, fine views extend across to the Cheviots; Newtown St Boswells is now the Headquarters for the Borders Regional Council. The green at nearby St Boswells has become famous over the

text continued on p. 14

Below: *Moffat;* **top right:** *Galashiels;* **bottom right:** *the Tweed near Dryburgh Abbey.*
Ci-dessous: *Moffat;* **à droite, en haut:** *Galashiels;* **en bas:** *la Tweed près de l'abbaye de Dryburgh.*
Unten: *Moffat;* **oben rechts:** *Galashiels;* **unten rechts:** *der Tweed bei der Dryburgh Abtei.*

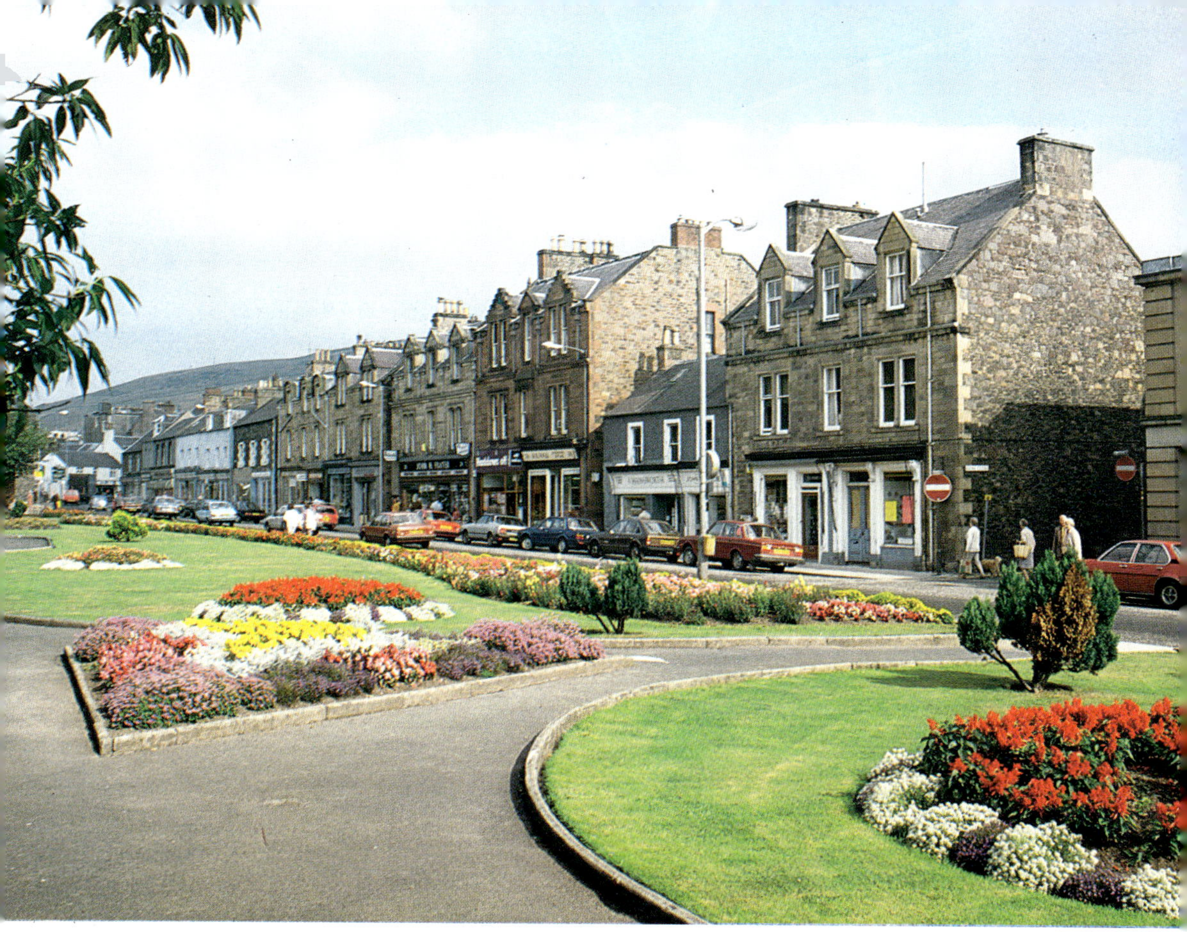

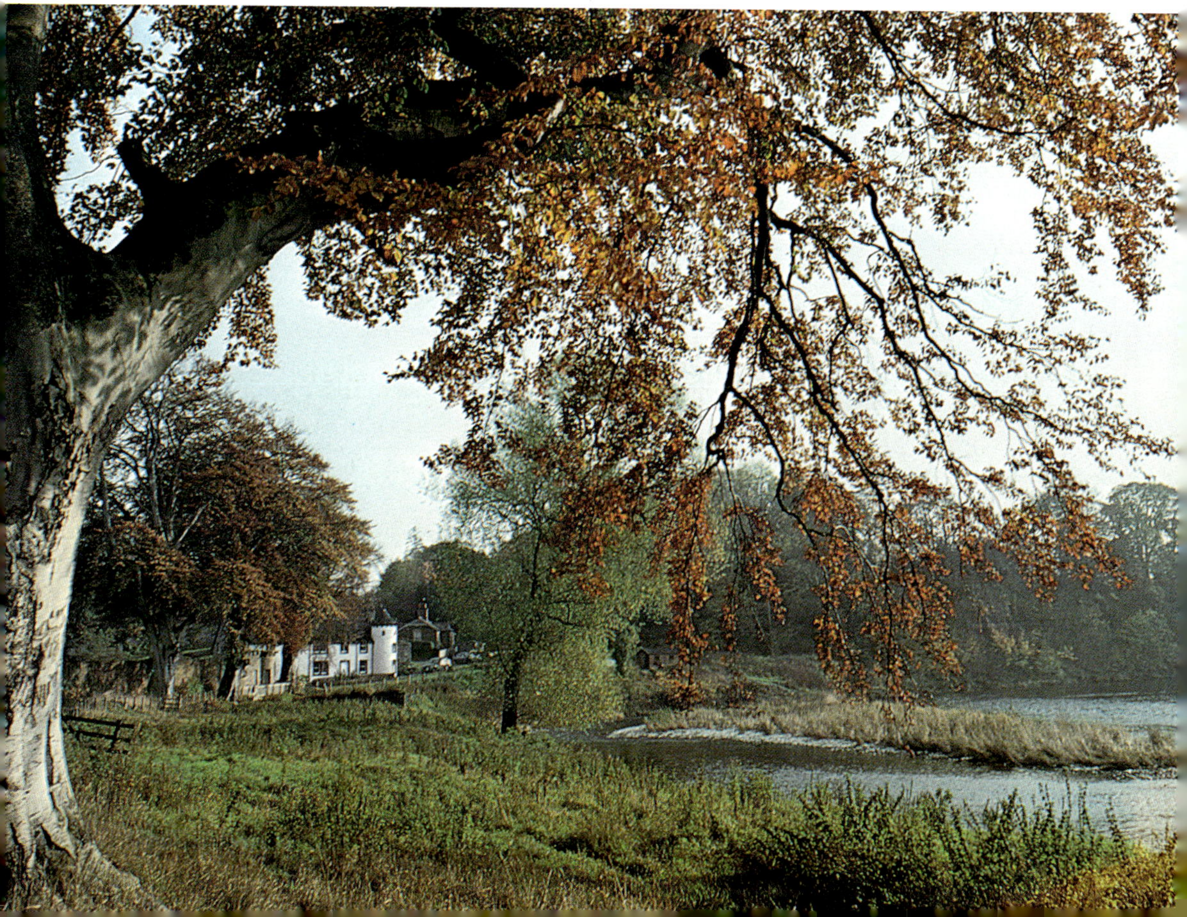

Abbeys of the Borders

The four great Border abbeys – Kelso, Melrose, Jedburgh and Dryburgh – make a triangular cluster in the centre of the region (C4, 5). Furthest to the west is Melrose (*right*), founded by Cistercian monks from Rievaulx, Yorkshire, in 1136, and consecrated ten years later. David I granted generous rights to lands and forests, grazing, wood and fishing, and further endowments made the abbey one of the wealthiest in the kingdom. However, it was sacked by the English in 1322 and 1385, and again in 1544 and 1545. From then on, materials were gradually removed by the townspeople for buildings elsewhere, and Melrose fell into ruin.

A little further east stands Dryburgh Abbey (*below*) in a peaceful valley setting beside the Tweed. Much of the community's living accommodation remains identifiable – the Chapter House in particular has beautiful interlaced ribbed arches embellishing the end wall and a fine barrel-vaulted ceiling – while in the north transept is Sir Walter Scott's grave. This Premonstratensian abbey was established in 1150. It was sacked in 1322, 1385, 1461 and 1523 by English Border raiders, and by the end of the sixteenth century it was in ruins.

Kelso Abbey (*below right*), is also by the Tweed, and was a reformed Benedictine (Tironensian) community founded by David I in 1128. It makes an appropriately impressive sight, for it was one of the largest and the second wealthiest of Scottish religious communities. It was finally destroyed in the mid sixteenth century by the English.

Jedburgh Abbey (*bottom*) is south of the previous three, on the Jed Water. David I also founded this, Augustinian, community, about 1138. Being so close to the Border it was continually raided and in the mid sixteenth century a final pillaging by the Earl of Hertford left it in ruins.

Information panels at all four abbeys provide interesting details to enhance the visitor's enjoyment.

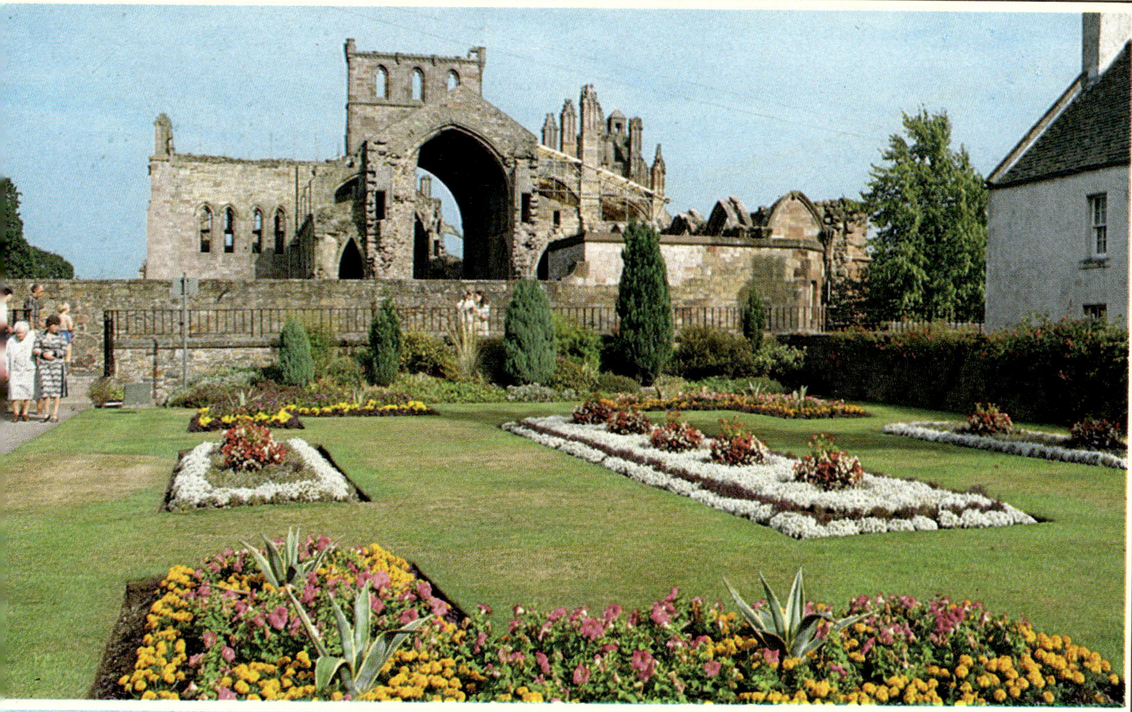

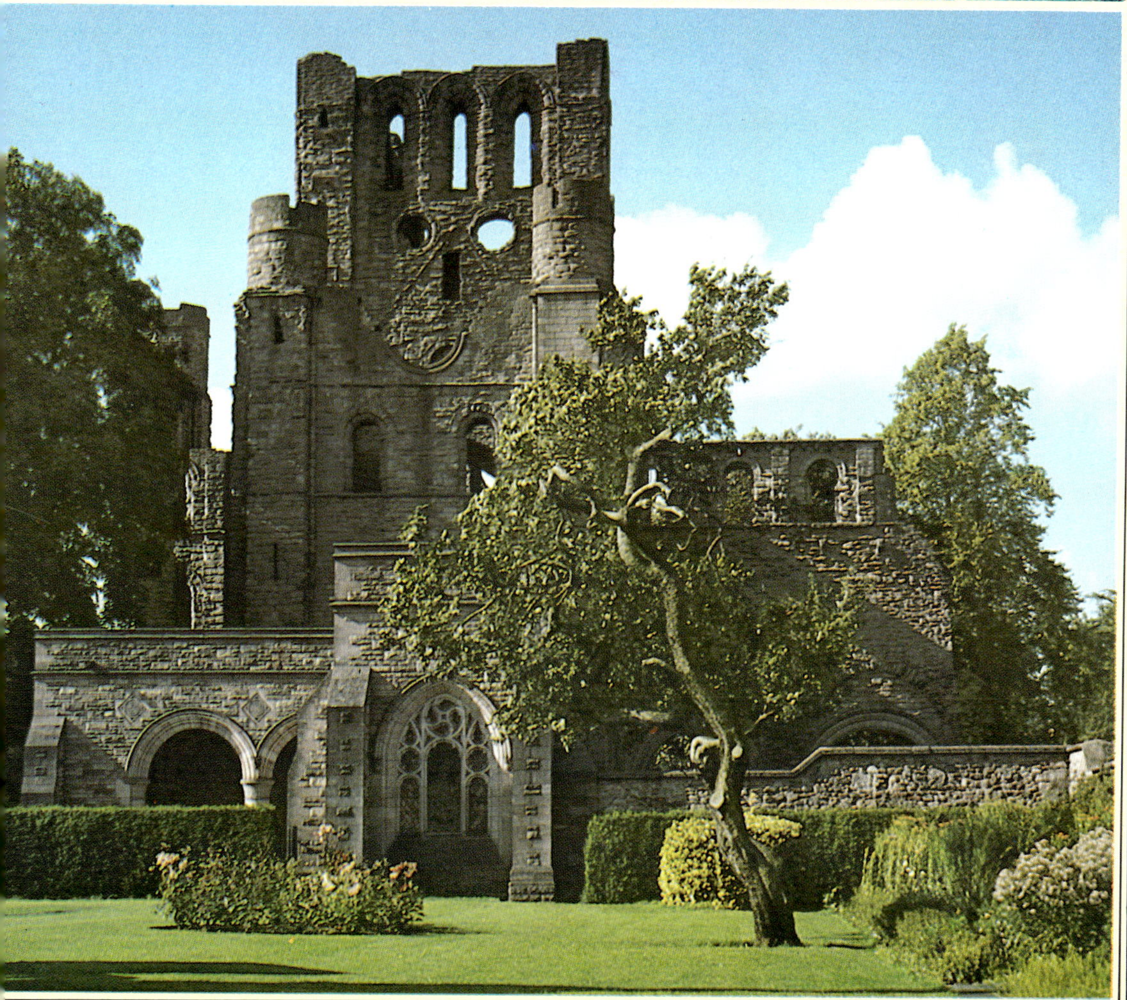

This page: *the harbour at Dunbar, just over the regional boundary in Lothian.*
Cette page: *le port de Dunbar, juste au-delà de la limite de la région du Lothian.*
Diese Seite: *Hafen in Dunbar nördlich der regionalen Grenze in Lothian.*

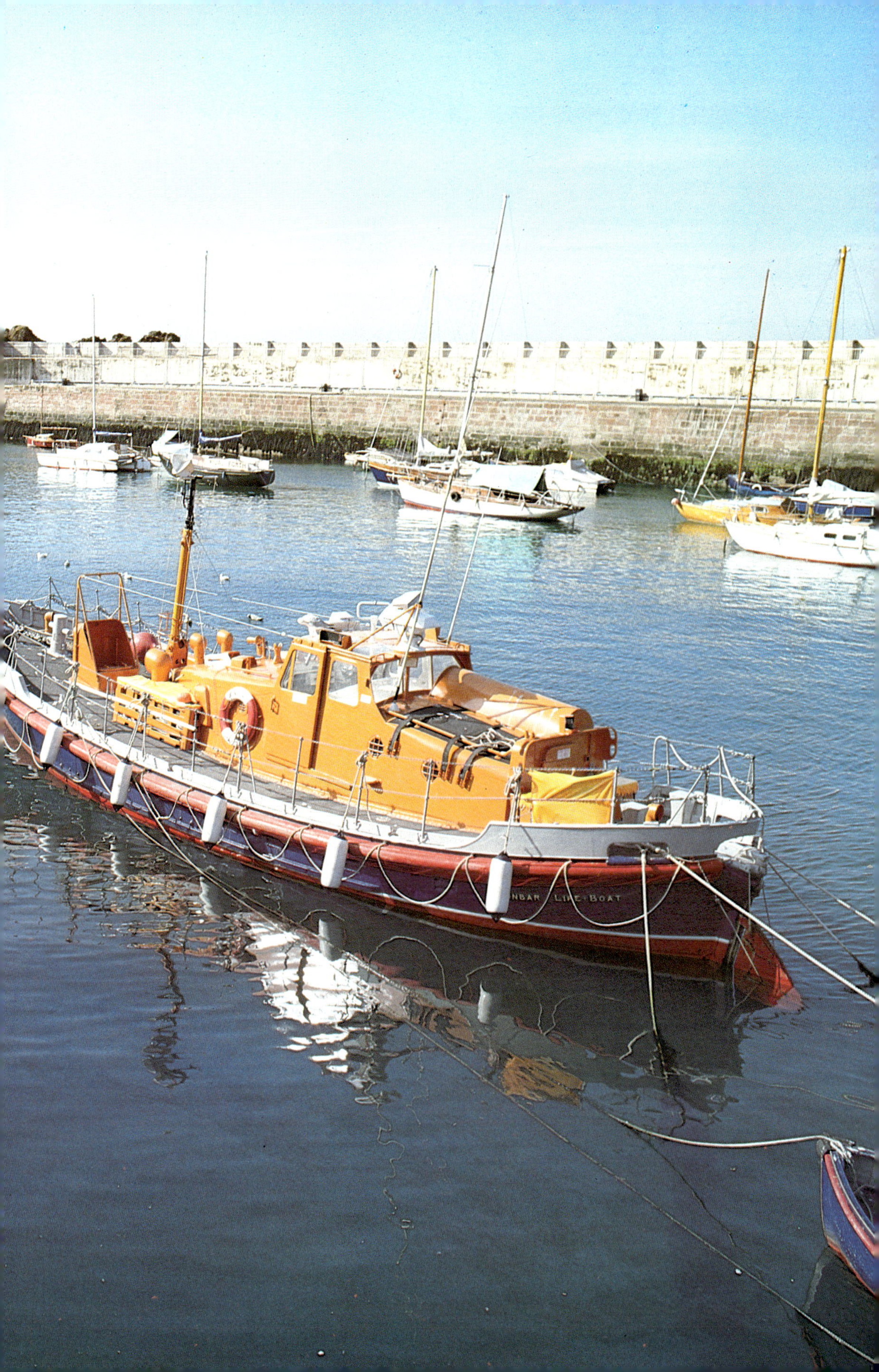
LIFE-BOAT

Towns, villages, countryside, continued

years as the venue for a gipsy fair each summer. From here there is a pleasant walk along the Tweed to Dryburgh Abbey. Newstead, to the north, is said to be Scotland's oldest inhabited village and lies over part of a Roman camp called 'Trimontium' after the three Eildon Hills. Further north is Earlston, home of the thirteenth-century poet and prophet Thomas the Rhymer – many of whose prophecies later came true.

Jedburgh (C5) is the third great abbey town. In addition to the abbey ruins, other interesting buildings include Mary Queen of Scots House, the Castle Jail and renovated houses on the main street. To the west of Jedburgh, Denholm (C4) clusters around a village green, rare in Scotland.

Last of the abbey towns is Kelso (C5), dominated also by Floors Castle; the town grew up around the abbey in medieval times and has cobbled streets with attractive eighteenth- and nineteenth-century frontages overlooking the square. Nearby was Roxburgh (now the name of a little village a few miles west) which was the capital of Scotland several times in early days, with a Royal Mint and its castle, today in ruins, the home of kings.

At Linton, to the south-east, is a carving of a dragon called the 'Linton Worm' over the main door of the church. Town Yetholm and Kirk Yetholm close by are at the end of the Pennine Way; Yetholm has close links with the Romanies, who once wintered here – the last Gipsy Queen died here in 1883.

Coldstream (B5), right on the Border, is famous for the regiment of guards raised in 1659 and is also a good angling centre. Greenlaw, to the west, was a main staging-post between Edinburgh and Newcastle.

Going north over Greenlaw Moor one reaches Duns (B5), famous as the home of the thirteenth-century scholar Duns Scotus. The architect and landscape-gardener Joseph Paxton, and Jim Clark, the racing driver, are other sons of Duns. The coast is reached at Eyemouth (A6), an ancient fishing town which still carries on its traditional trade. Coldingham nearby has the ruins of a great priory, while the little fishing village of St Abb's, just below St Abb's Head (a National Nature Reserve with important sea-bird breeding colonies) was once a smuggling centre. The historic walled town of Berwick-on-Tweed is not far away; it frequently changed hands between Scots and English before settling south of the Border.

Above: *North Berwick, a little farther up the coast from Dunbar;* **left:** *St Abb's, a fishing village, is sheltered by St Abb's Head.*
Ci-dessus: *North Berwick, au Nord de Dunbar le long de la côte;* **à gauche:** *St Abb's, port de pêche abrité par St Abb's Head.*
Oben: *North Berwick etwas nördlicher von Dunbar an der Küste gelegen;* **links:** *St. Abb's, ein Fischerdorf, liegt im Schutz von St. Abb's Head.*

THE SCOTTISH BORDERS

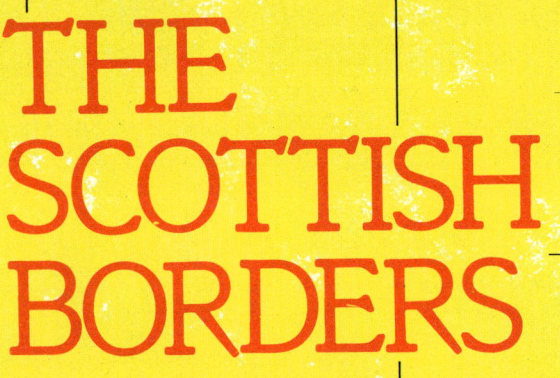

Places of Interest

1. Tweedsmuir – Crook Inn
2, 3. James Hogg Monuments
4. Dryhope Tower
5. Dawyck
6. Kailzie
7. Neidpath Castle
8. Tweeddale Museum, Peebles
9. Traquair House Innerleithen, Traquair and Glen Museum
10. Scottish Museum of Woollen Textiles, Walkerburn
11. Bowhill
12. Halliwell's House Museum, Selkirk
13. Wilton Lodge Museum, Hawick
14. Hermitage Castle
15. Mary Queen of Scots House, Jedburgh
16. Castle Jail, Jedburgh
17. Woodland Centre, near Jedburgh
18. Melrose Motor Museum
19. Priorwood Gardens
20. Abbotsford
21. Galashiels Museum
22. Thirlestane Castle
23. Border Country Life Museum, Lauder
24. Greenknowe Tower
25. Mellerstain
26. Smailholm Tower
27. Floors Castle
28. Coldstream Museum
29. The Hirsel
30. Jim Clark Room, Duns
31. Manderston
32. Ayton Castle
33. Eyemouth Museum

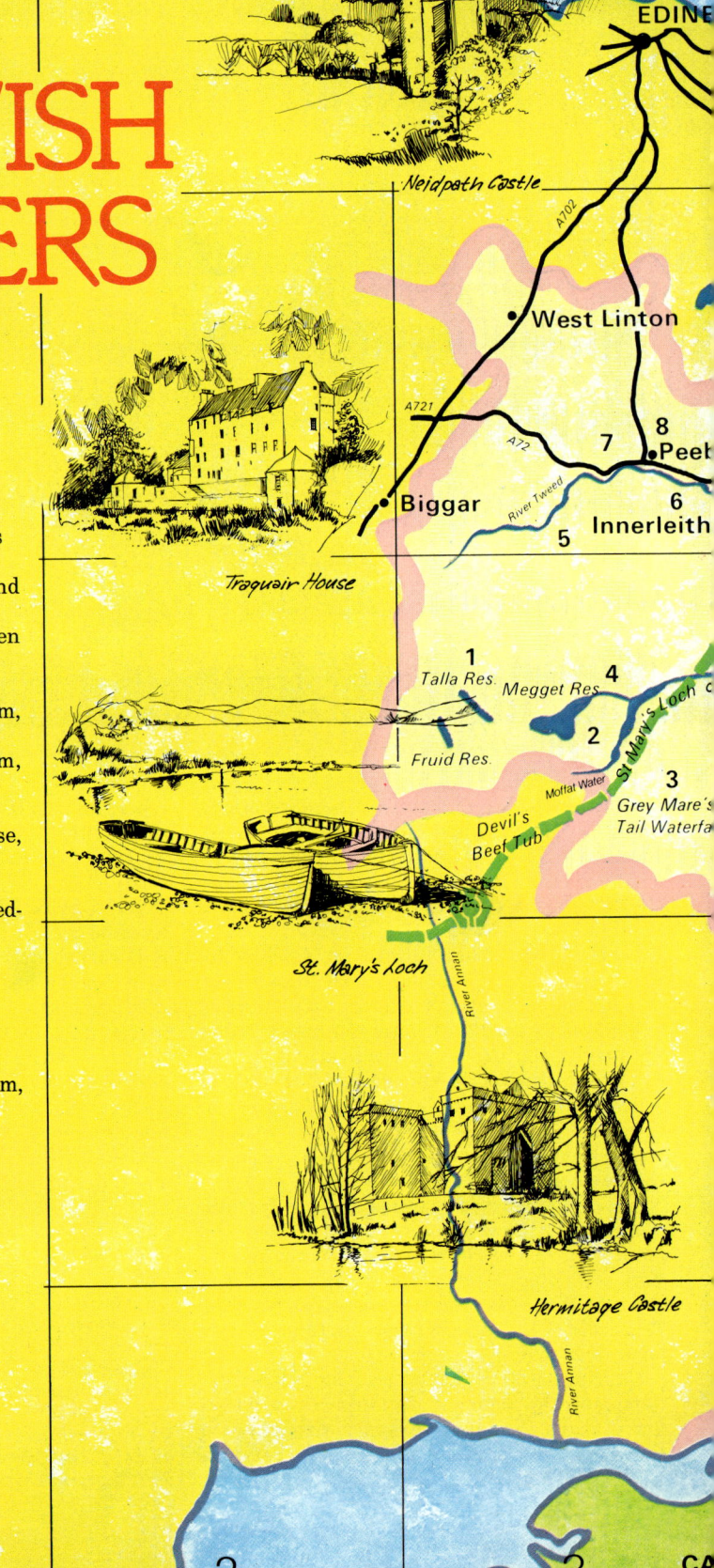

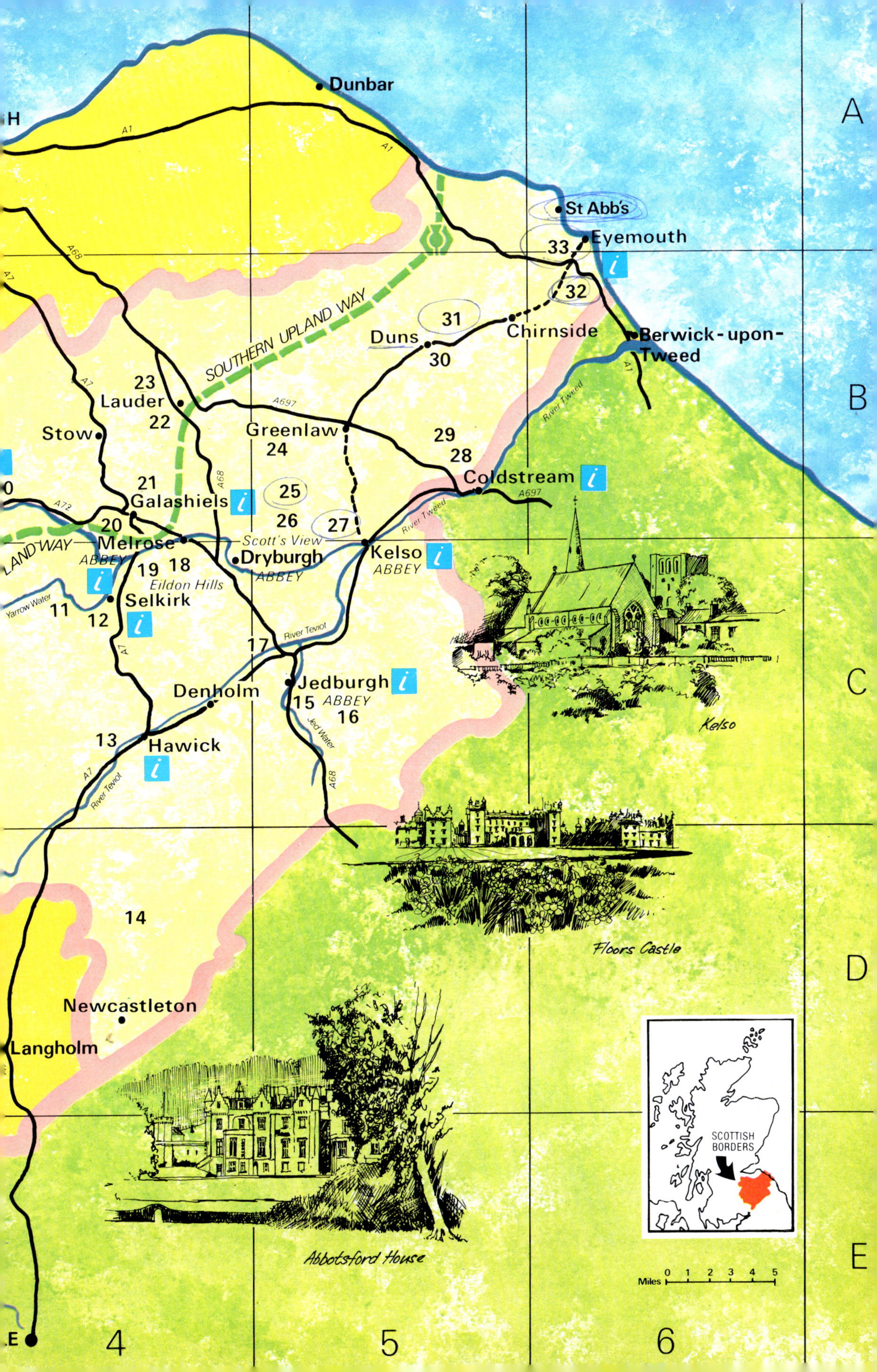

Dunbar
A
H
A1
A1
St Abb's
Eyemouth
33
32
31
Chirnside
Berwick-upon-Tweed
Duns
30
SOUTHERN UPLAND WAY
A68
A7
A7
23
Lauder
22
A697
Greenlaw
24
Stow
29
28
B
Coldstream
A697
River Tweed
21
Galashiels
A68
25
26
27
A72
20
Melrose
Scott's View
River Tweed
LAND WAY
ABBEY
18
19
Dryburgh
ABBEY
Kelso
ABBEY
Eildon Hills
Yarrow Water
11
Selkirk
12
A7
17
River Teviot
Denholm
Jedburgh
ABBEY
15
16
C
13
Hawick
Jed Water
A7
River Teviot
A68
Kelso
Floors Castle
14
D
Newcastleton
Langholm
SCOTTISH BORDERS
Abbotsford House
E
Miles 0 1 2 3 4 5
E
4
5
6

Castles, Houses and Gardens

When deciding which historic castle, stately mansion or pleasant garden to visit in the Borders, the choice is almost overwhelming. With its turbulent history of Border raids and battles between Scots and English, it is not surprising that the countryside was well defended with castles and peel towers; most are now in ruins, but enough survives of many such fortifications to impress the visitor with their strength. Some of the great houses also started life as defensive structures but were altered and enriched over succeeding centuries to become the comfortable homes seen today. Others were built in more peaceful times and show elegant Georgian taste, Victorian romance or Edwardian magnificence. Many of these mansions are set in beautiful gardens and parkland, which adds greatly to the visitor's enjoyment; there are also other gardens and woodlands to enjoy which have been lovingly tended over many years and welcome visitors. NB – It is wise to contact the appropriate local Tourist Information Office to check when the castle, house or garden you wish to see will be open.

Set on the banks of the Tweed just outside Peebles (B3) is medieval Neidpath Castle; once a Fraser stronghold, the castle dates from the early fourteenth century and has walls twelve feet thick. From the top there are magnificent views over the Tweed. To the east of Peebles lie Kailzie Gardens, which include herbaceous and shrub borders and formal beds, woodland walks and greenhouses. For tree-lovers, a visit to Dawyck Arboretum, south-west of the town, will be rewarding; the bulbs in spring and the flowering shrubs are set off against a background of many unusual trees.

Traquair House, near Innerleithen (B4), claims to be the oldest inhabited house in Scotland; since the twelfth century twenty-seven Scottish and English monarchs have stayed at Traquair and among the collections of furniture, porcelain, glass and miniatures are several items closely associated with royal visitors, including embroidery by Mary Queen of Scots. Traquair is unique among private

Left, top: *Floors Castle;* **second:** *Thirlestane Castle;* **third:** *Traquair House;* **bottom:** *Hermitage Castle.*
A gauche du haut en bas: *Floors Castle, Thirlestane Castle, Traquair House, Hermitage Castle.*
Links oben: *Burg Floors;* **2. Bild:** *Burg Thirlestane;* **3. Bild:** *Traquair House;* **unten;** *Burg Hermitage.*

houses in having its own licensed brew-house, dating from the eighteenth century.

South-west of Traquair, near St Mary's Loch (C3), stands Dryhope Tower, a massive peel tower which is associated with an ancestress of Sir Walter Scott – Mary Scott, the 'Flower of Yarrow', born here in 1550. There is also a Scott connection at ruined Newark Castle, dating from the fifteenth century and near Selkirk (C4), which once belonged to the Scotts of Buccleuch and which Sir Walter used as a setting for *The Lay of the Last Minstrel*.

Nearby is Bowhill, a graceful Georgian mansion set in lovely gardens, with superb collections of paintings and French furniture. Bowhill is the headquarters of the Scott family, being the home of the Duke of Buccleuch and Queensberry, and there are relics of Sir Walter Scott to be seen here. Children will particularly enjoy the adventure woodland play area.

The town of Melrose (C4) not only has Priorwood Gardens, adjacent to the abbey and specialising in flowers which can be dried, but also, just to the west, Scott's beloved Abbotsford. Built between 1817 and 1822, the house contains Scott's collection of historic relics, his atmospheric study and much else to enjoy and discover about this great writer and poet.

Thirlestane Castle, at Lauder (B4), is much older, with a keep of about 1590, although extensive additions were made in about 1840. The plan of the keep is unusual for a Scottish mansion house, having corner towers and stair turrets; inside, many of the rooms have beautiful plaster ceilings and panelled walls. The recently opened Border Country Life Museum, and walks in the surrounding woodlands are additional attractions.

Kelso (C5) is particularly well-off when it comes to castles and houses, having no less than five nearby. The largest and grandest is Floors Castle – probably the largest inhabited house in Scotland. The original house was designed by William Adam in 1721, but it was

Above: *Bowhill;* **below:** *Mellerstain.*
Ci-dessus: *Bowhill;* **ci-dessous:** *Mellerstain.*
Oben: *Bowhill;* **unten:** *Mellerstain.*

greatly enlarged and embellished with spires, domes and turrets by William Playfair in 1841. French furniture, tapestries and Chinese and European porcelain are among the many fine works of art on display here. Not far away are the ruins of Roxburgh Castle, once lived in by kings of Scotland. Two fine fifteenth-century tower-houses – Smailholm and Greenknowe – are also in the neighbourhood.

In complete contrast is Mellerstain, a magnificent Adam house set among terraced gardens. William Adam designed the wings in 1725 and the main block was added forty years later by Robert Adam, who was also responsible for the interior décor and ceilings, still to be seen, which set off admirably the fine furniture and paintings.

In the east of the region at Coldstream (B5) stands The Hirsel, home of Lord Home; although the house is not open to visitors, its beautiful grounds and Dundock Wood can be explored. At Duns (B5), to the north, will be found Manderston, described as 'the swan-song of the great classical house'. Edwardian in date, though Georgian in inspiration, no expense was spared, above or below stairs, to create a supremely comfortable country mansion – the silver staircase and superbly equipped servants' quarters are especially memorable.

At the opposite extreme, in date and grandeur, is Edinshall Broch, set in the Lammermuir Hills near Abbey St Bathans. This was constructed in the Iron Age, only the base being visible today. Such brochs are among the earliest defensive structures to be seen in Scotland.

Ayton Castle, near Eyemouth (A6), is different again – dating from 1846, it was designed by Gillespie Graham and represents Victorian Scottish Baronial architecture at its most confident.

Most southerly of the Border castles is Hermitage Castle, near Newcastleton (D4). This well-preserved but severe-looking medieval keep stands overlooking bleak fells. It was to this castle that Mary Queen of Scots rode from Jedburgh to see the wounded Earl of Bothwell in 1566; after her exhausting ride she developed a fever and nearly died.

A visit to these Border castles and houses will bring to life the way in which people lived in past centuries, and provide an interesting, entertaining and enjoyable day out in the beautiful Borders countryside.

Main picture: *Manderston;* **inset:** *Greenknowe Tower.*
Grande photo: *Manderston;* **encadré:** *Greenknowe Tower.*
Großes Bild: *Manderston;* **daneben:** *Greenknowe Turm.*

Border Forests

Centuries ago, the countryside of the Borders was thickly wooded, with Scots pine, oak, wych elm, alder, ash and rowan, but gradually the land was cleared for agricultural use, animals grazed down young seedling trees, the wood was burnt for fuel and by the early nineteenth century little trace of the great natural forests remained. However, as early as the sixteenth and seventeenth centuries some far-sighted lairds established plantations on their lands, and this continued on a larger scale in the eighteenth and nineteenth centuries.

The establishment of the Forestry Commission in 1919 saw the beginning of large-scale afforestation to provide timber for many different industrial uses. As well as the Commission's own forests, there has been considerable co-operation from private landowners in planting new woodlands.

Today, seven forested areas throughout the country have been made Forest Parks for recreational use, and the Border Forest Park is one of these. In addition, other forests have been increasingly made available to visitors in recent years, examples in the Borders including Glentress (B3), Elibank and Traquair (B3, C3), Lammermuir (B6) and Craik (C4, D4) Forests.

Facilities for visitors are wide-ranging. Walking is encouraged, with waymarked trails and information about interesting things to be seen along the path, and there are established picnic places. Cars are generally barred –

except for a few designated forest drives – so the forests provide a haven for wildlife: for the birdwatcher there are goldcrests, coal tits, wrens, robins, dunnock, woodcock, crossbills, siskins (*top left*), sparrowhawks, kestrels, barn owls, tawny owls, etc. Animals include the delightful red squirrels, foxes and roe deer (*above*) while among the many insects are Orange-tip, Scotch Argus (*below left*) and Green-hairstreak (*centre*) butterflies and Purple Emperor moths. Other pursuits encouraged include hill-climbing, fishing and riding (by permit).

Visitor Centres have displays showing different aspects of the forests and stock Commission publications; check in advance for opening times.

En face, en haut à gauche: *tarin des Aulnes;* **en bas:** *Scotch Argus;* **à droite, en bas:** *Green Hairstreak;* **ci-dessus:** *chevreuil;* **en bas:** « Braw Lads Day » *à Galashiels.*
Gegenüberl. Seite, oben links: *Siskin;* **unten links:** *Scotch Argus;* **unten rechts:** *Grüne Haarsträhne;* **oben:** *Rehkitz;* **unten rechts:** *Galashiels Braw Lads Day.*

Common Ridings

Annual festivals on horseback are an exciting feature of Border life, descending from the days when Borderers rode out to preserve their boundaries and protect them from encroachment. Selkirk's Common Riding, in June, starts with parties the night before, then on the day itself with a procession to meet the Standard Bearer (who must be a souter) and his cavalcade. The horsemen ride at a cracking pace to the top of Three Brethren Cairn before returning to the town for the Casting of the Colour. At Hawick's Common Riding, also in June, the cavalcade is led by the Cornet, and includes a full-blooded gallop celebrating the return of Hawick callants (youths) from routing the English in 1514. Jedburgh's Redeswire Ride takes place in July, and ends with Border Games. (Jedburgh also plays an ancient and vigorous version of hand-ba' through the streets at Candlemas and Easter E'en, the two teams – Uppies and Doonies – coming from the upper and lower town.) The Braw Lad's Gathering (*right*) at Galashiels in June is of relatively recent date, but celebrates another English defeat of centuries ago: soldiers who stopped to pick wild plums were attacked and routed. The town's motto is 'Soor Plums'!

23

Museums and other places to visit

The following listings include many, but by no means all, of the museums and other places of interest which welcome visitors. In addition, it has not been possible to give comprehensive opening times and dates, as these are subject to change. Please contact local Tourist Information Offices for opening times, and also for details of other things to do and places to go.

MUSEUMS

Border Country Life Museum, Thirlestane Castle, Lauder (B4). Covers many aspects of life in the Borders, including veterinary display, reconstruction of a carpenter's shop, farming equipment, etc.

John Buchan Centre, Broughton, Nr. Biggar (B2). Tells the story of John Buchan's life and work, as novelist, biographer and Governor-General of Canada.

Jim Clark Room, Duns (B5). Trophies and memorabilia of the former world motor racing champion, born at Duns.

Coldstream Museum, Coldstream (B5). Contains items associated with the Coldstream Guards, raised in the town in 1659 and other local history exhibits.

Eyemouth Museum, Eyemouth (A6). Folk-life museum with particular emphasis on the local fishing industry and Eastern Berwickshire's history. Based in a converted Georgian church (*below right*).

Galashiels Museum, Nether Mill, Galashiels (B4). Shows the development of the town as a textile centre, and includes guided mill tour.

Halliwell's House Museum, Selkirk (C4). Re-creation of past role as home and ironmonger's shop. Also, local history section.

The Hirsel Estate Exhibition Centre, Coldstream (B5). How a large estate is managed, nature walks, farm equipment, stuffed birds.

Innerleithen, Traquair and Glen Museum, Innerleithen (B4). Local history museum.

Jedburgh Castle Jail, Jedburgh (C5). Displays reconstruct life in a 'reformed' jail in the early nineteenth century.

Mary Queen of Scots House, Jedburgh (C5). Museum with relics of the Queen, housed in a sixteenth-century bastel house where she is believed to have stayed in 1566 (*centre right*).

Melrose Motor Museum, Melrose (C4). Collection of vintage cars (*top right*), motorcycles, bicycles and associated items.

Scottish Museum of Woollen Textiles, Walkerburn (B4). Shows the history of textile

Right: *the Grey Mare's Tail waterfall.*
A droite: *chutes dites « queue de la jument grise ».*
Rechts: *Grauer Stutenschwanzwasserfall.*

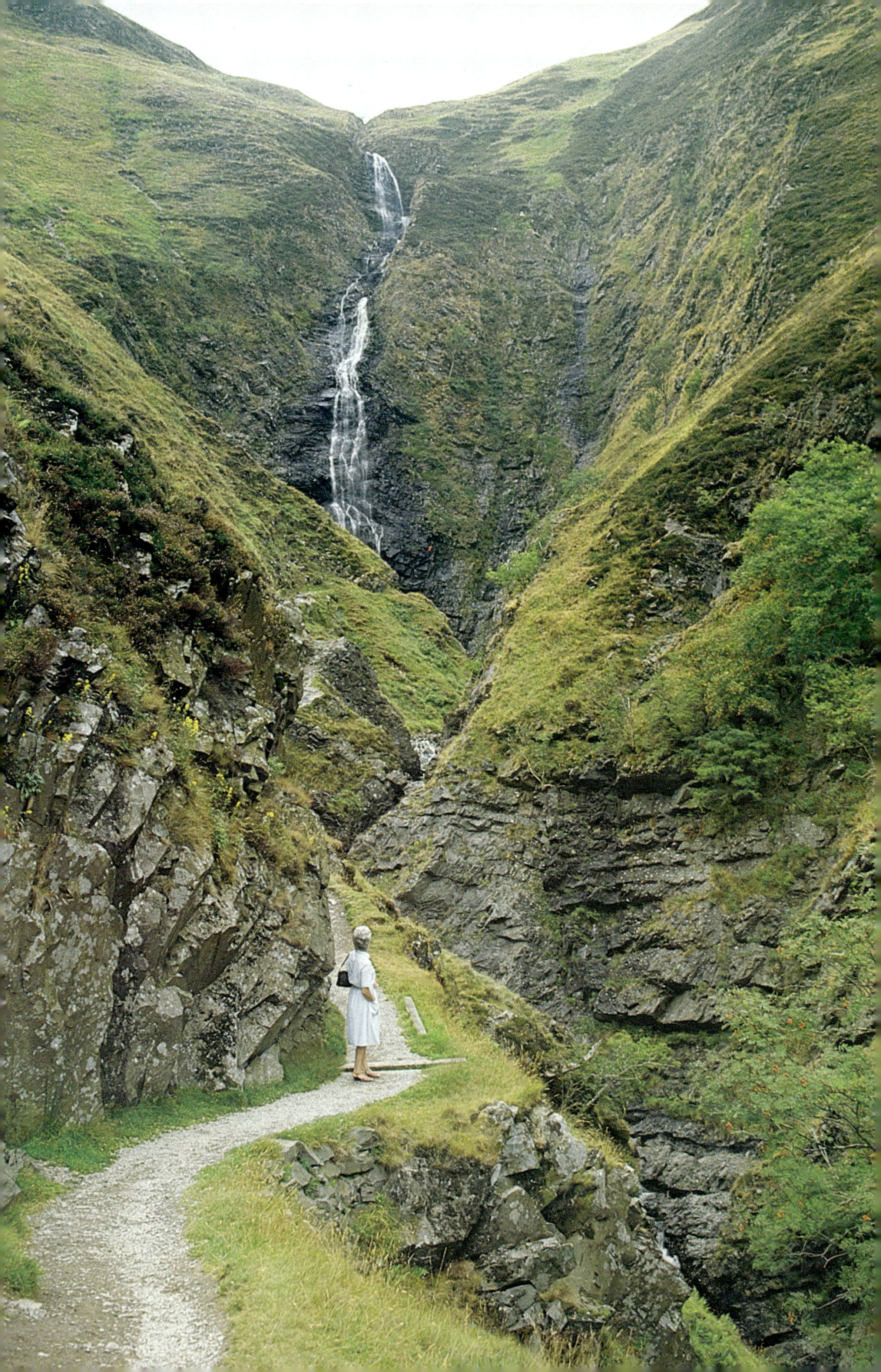

production from cottage industry to full mechanisation. Includes reconstructions of weaving-shed and cottage interior, information about methods of weaving, dyeing, the influence of fashion, etc.

Selkirk Town Hall, Selkirk (C4). Sir Walter Scott's Sheriff Court-room with his bench and chair, and items belonging to other famous people associated with Selkirk, for example, James Hogg (shepherd poet and friend of Sir Walter), the explorer Mungo Park, and Robert Burns.

Tweeddale Museum, Peebles (B3). Museum of local history housed in Chambers Institute, given to the town by publisher William Chambers, born in the town.

Wilton Lodge Museum, Hawick (C4). Collection of local and Border items, art gallery, and natural history collection. Set in parkland with riverside walks, gardens, etc.

OTHER PLACES TO VISIT

The Woodland Centre, Jedburgh (C5). Exhibits about woodlands and their commercial and recreational roles. Woodland walks.

Craft Workshops. For details of the many workshops and sales outlets in the Borders, see *A Visitor's Guide to Scottish Craft Workshops* published jointly by the Scottish Development Agency and the Scottish Tourist Board.

Textile Mills. Several mills welcome visitors and offer tours, and details of these are obtainable from local Tourist Information Centres at Galashiels, Hawick and Selkirk. There are also many shops selling Borders-produced textiles throughout the region, which make an ideal souvenir of your visit.

Border Festivals. Most of the Border towns hold a Common Riding or other festival annually. These include Coldstream Civic Week, Duns Summer Festival, Galashiels Braw Lads Gathering, Hawick Common Riding, Jedburgh Callants Festival, Kelso Civic Week, Lauder Common Riding, Melrose Festival Week, Peebles Beltane Week, Selkirk Common Riding, West Linton Whipman Play, Eyemouth Herring Queen Festival, Innerleithen St Ronan's Games. Dates of these festivals vary from year to year, but most occur in the summer months and you may well find one taking place somewhere nearby during your visit to the Borders; once again, consult the local Tourist Information Office.

St Mary's Loch (C3). A very pleasant day can be spent in the neighbourhood of this beautiful loch, walking, picnicking and visiting the nearby reservoirs, the Grey Mare's Tail waterfall and the Devil's Beef Tub, where stolen cattle were once hidden. Sailing also takes place on the loch.

OVER THE BORDERS BORDER – Places within easy reach.

John Muir Country Park, Dunbar (A5). 1,667 acres to explore on the Berwickshire coast, with a waymarked Nature Trail (follow the green duck's feet!), sandy beaches, rock pools, and varied bird, insect and plant life.

Ford and Etal Estates, Cornhill-on-Tweed. Operating water-driven corn-mill, craft shops, Lady Waterford Hall (with murals painted by Lady Waterford in the nineteenth century, using local people as models), smithy, etc.

Top: *the Scottish Museum of Woollen Textiles, Walkerburn, braces the industry's history;* **left:** *the Devil's Beef Tub;* **right:** *sailing enthusiasts enjoy St Mary's Loch;* **above right:** *Wilton Lodge Museum, Hawick.*

En haut: *le musée des lainages de Walkerburn retrace l'histoire de cette industrie;* **à gauche:** *le « Devil's Beef Tub »;* **à droite:** *amateurs de voile sur le loch St Mary's;* **ci-dessus, à droite:** *le musée de Wilton Lodge à Hawick.*

Oben: *Schottisches Museum für Wollstoffe, Walkerburn;* **links:** *Teufelsrindertopf;* **rechts:** *Segelbegeisterte auf St. Mary's Loch;* **oben rechts:** *Wilton Lodge Museum, Hawick.*

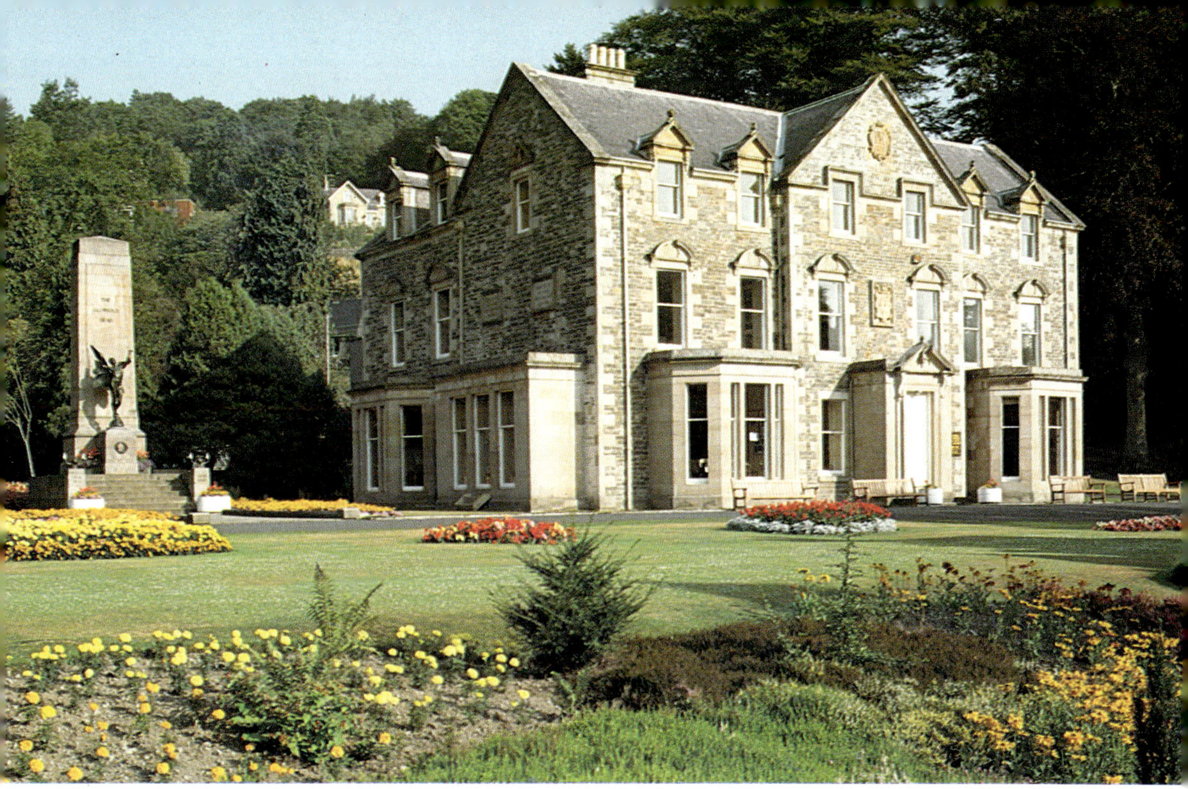

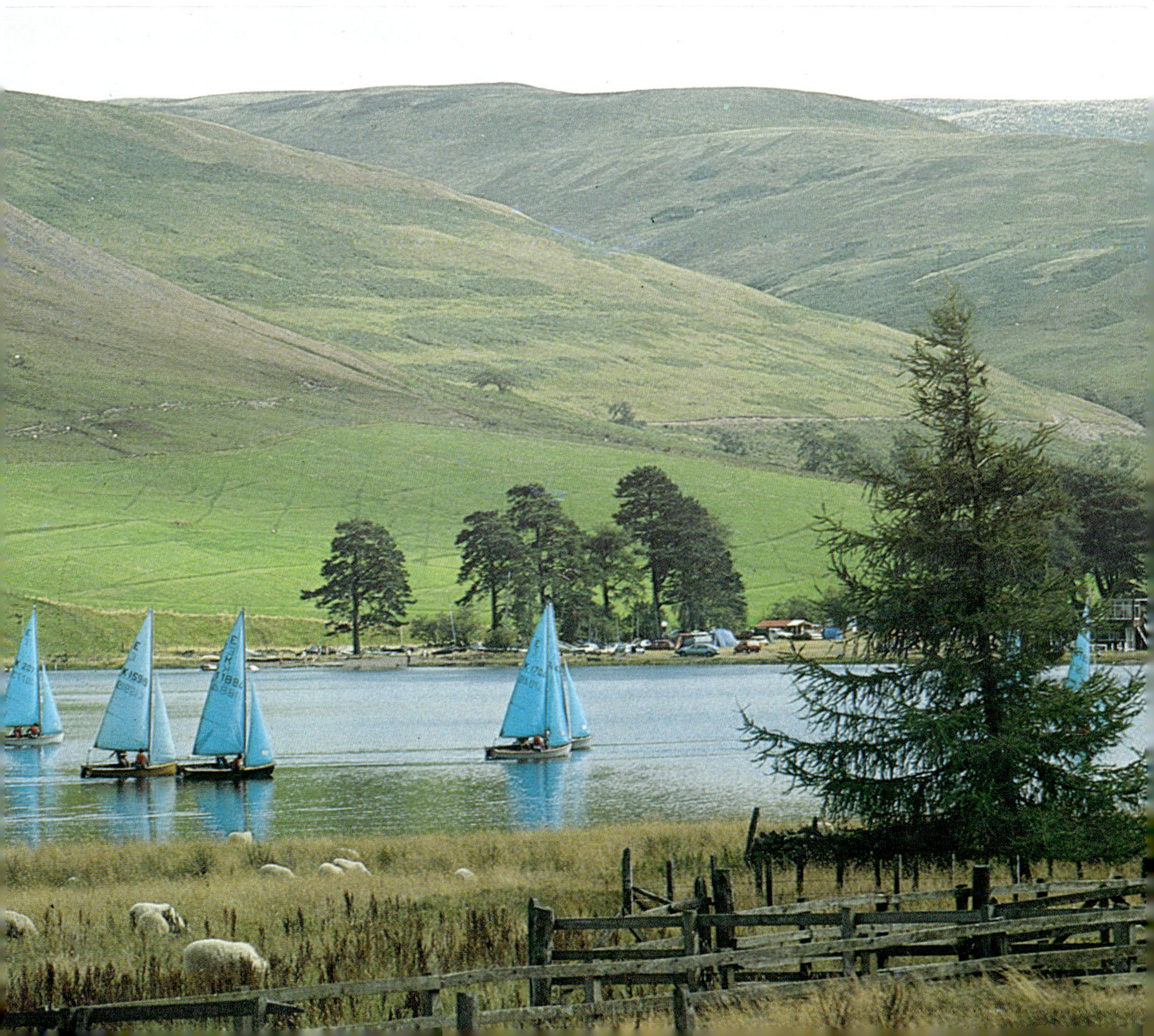

Walking in the Borders

The countryside of the Borders offers a wide variety of contrasting scenery – hills and river valleys, moorland and pastures, forests and ancient towns – which can ideally be enjoyed on foot. Walkers are welcomed throughout the area, with signposted paths and specialist publications available to guide them, and routes range from the challenging Southern Upland Way (see opposite page) to afternoon rambles for the family.

For the experienced walker, the many hill ranges with evocative names – Cheviots, Tweedsmuirs, Pentlands, Lammermuirs and Moorfoots – offer superb views as the reward for a long hike up over moorland and crag. The Countryside Ranger Service at the Borders Regional Council (Regional Headquarters, Newtown St Boswells, TD6 0SA) can give information about long-distance walks among the hills.

Less ambitious but full of interest are the Town Walks established in many of the Border towns, which make use of local footpaths and rights of way to explore less-frequented parts, and sometimes unusual and unexpected aspects, of each town. Information on these can be found at local Tourist Information Centres.

So far as walks in the countryside are concerned, in addition to the facilities provided by the Forestry Commission (for which see the article on Border Forests) there are many routes to and around places of interest (abbeys, stately mansions, ruined castles), some of which are set beside tranquil rivers, others amid green or wooded landscapes, which provide a goal during the walk. There are also coastal footpaths where the scenery and birdlife make a ramble richly rewarding. Once again, local Tourist Information Centres or the Scottish Borders Tourist Board can give details, and they also stock a useful series of publications for the walker.

Note: It is most important to wear good boots and sensible, warm clothing when walking in the hills. Carry a spare jumper, a food supply, maps and a compass. Weather conditions can change rapidly and unpredictably, and it is better to be prepared.

Below: *Kelso;* **above right:** *back-packing along the Southern Upland Way;* **below right:** *map showing the route of the Way.*
Ci-dessous: *Kelso;* **ci-dessus, à droite:** *randonneurs sur le Southern Upland Way;* **ci-dessous, à droite:** *tracé de ce sentier de Grande Randonnée.*
Unten: *Kelso;* **rechts, oben:** *Wandern im südlichen Hochland;* **rechts, unten:** *Wanderkarte mit Route des Hochlandes.*

The Southern Upland Way

The Southern Upland Way is a long-distance footpath running for 212 miles (340 km) from Portpatrick on the west coast to Cockburnspath (A5) on the east coast. It passes through Dumfries and Galloway, Strathclyde and, for the eastern half of the route, through the heart of the Borders.

The Way makes use of many existing paths and tracks, some in use for many hundreds of years: coffin roads (along which coffins were once taken for burial), drove roads, military roads, forest roads, lochside paths, trackbeds of disused railways and many other established routes have all been incorporated, while new paths have been constructed where necessary.

In the south of Scotland, the direction of river valleys and therefore of roads and railways, is predominantly north–south. This means that the Southern Upland Way, passing from west to east, is not an 'easy' route, despite not being in the Highlands, because for much of the time it is necessary to walk up and down quite steep gradients. It is important to be properly equipped, with good boots, warm clothing, a food reserve, maps and a compass.

An excellent guide, *The Southern Upland Way* by Ken Andrew, published by HMSO in two sections, price £5·95 per section (including a separate, well-detailed map with each). It is available from all nine Scottish Borders Tourist Information Centres, and good bookshops.

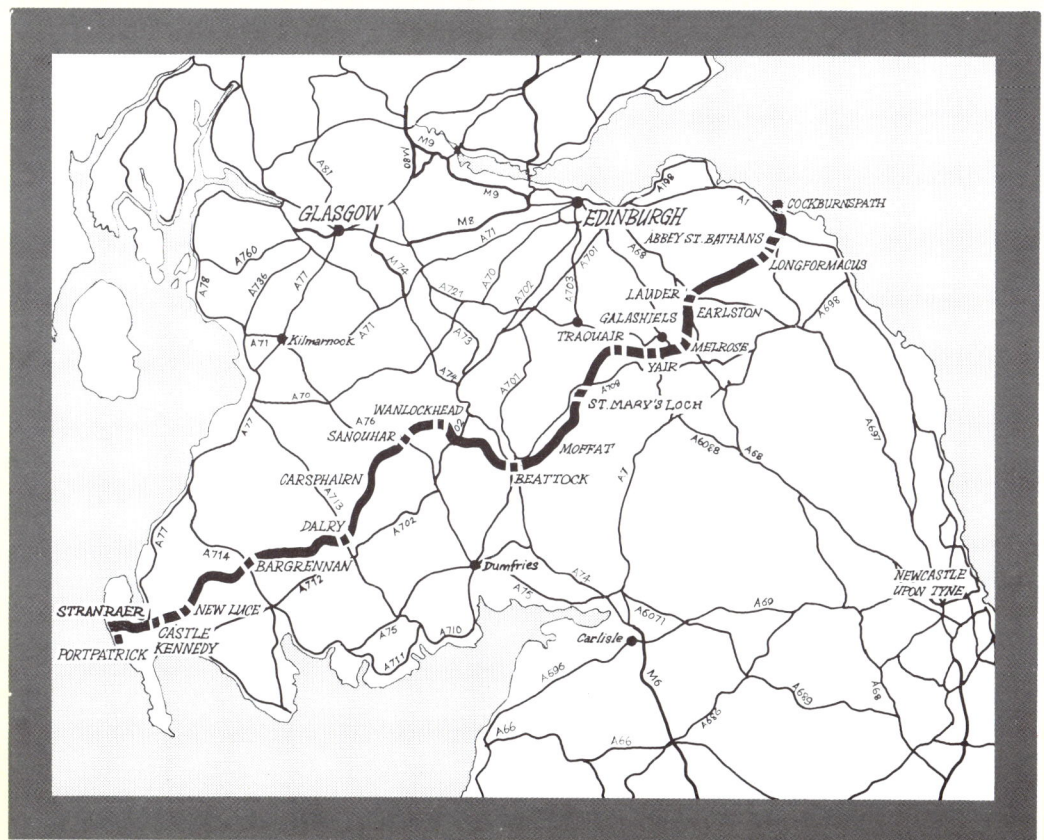

The Woollen Industry

The Borders and the woollen industry meet together in many people's minds with one word – 'tweed'. This name for a particular type of cloth arose from a misreading of the dialect word 'tweel' (twill) – unfamiliar south of the Border – for the name of the well-known river, and ever since the cloth and the river running through the countryside where it is woven have shared the same name.

Wool has been spun and woven in the Borders for centuries: the monks of the four great abbeys – Melrose, Kelso, Dryburgh and Jedburgh – all kept great flocks of sheep, exporting some wool to the Continent but also teaching local people the technique of weaving developed in the monks' native Flanders and northern France.

Weaving was originally a cottage industry, carried out in attic rooms or in weaving-sheds attached to the main building. The Scottish Museum of Woollen Textiles at Walkerburn (B4) shows a reconstruction of a weaving-shed and a cottage room, with spinning-wheel prominent among its furnishings. Cloth

produced on the cottagers' looms was sent for 'waulking' (finishing by shrinking cloth to the right thickness) to waulk-mills – Galashiels had two such mills by the sixteenth century.

In the seventeenth century, weavers from Selkirk, Hawick and Melrose in turn came together to create a craft, and in the eighteenth century the first corporation of woollen manufacturers was formed in Galashiels. This caused an explosion in the population of the town and in its number of looms. In 1777 Galashiels had 600 inhabitants, thirty looms and three waulk-mills. By 1827 there were 2000 people living there, 175 mills and thirty-four woollen manufacturers. Hawick grew in a similar way at this time, becoming a major centre of the knitting industry. Despite ups and downs (for example the depression after the Napoleonic Wars) spinning, weaving and knitting have remained the main Border industries to the present day.

The Borders proved ideal for the industrialisation of textile production, because of the abundant supplies of wool and soft water – for waulking the cloth and driving the mills. Surprisingly, the processes used today for spinning and weaving are essentially the same as those used by cottagers centuries ago, despite mechanisation.

The first stage in making cloth is **sorting** – classifying the fleeces as they come from the suppliers; neck and shoulder wool is the best, tail and hind-leg wool the least good. The wool is then **scoured** – washed and dried, teased out ('teased' coming from the teasels once used for the process), oiled for ease of handling and carded – combed so that the strands can be wound on to bobbins. From the bobbins the wool is **spun** – drawn out and twisted into a thread of the required thickness and strength (the more twists, the stronger the wool). Next the wool is **dyed** (this may also be done after scouring). Nowadays, chemical dyes have been developed but once the industry was dependent on natural sources – green from broom or

Below: *setting the reproduction Red Gordon tartan on a conventional shuttle-loom, at Peter Anderson's mill, Galashiels.*
Ci-dessous: *montage d'un tartan Red Gordon sur un métier à tisser traditionnel à Galashiels.*
Unten: *Herrichten zum Weben des Red Gordon Schottenmusters auf dem traditionellen Webrahmen in Peter Andersons Weberei, Galashiels.*